The Love Correction

12 Tools for Overcoming Trauma

VICTORIA HARDY

PUBLISHER

United States

Dedication

This book is dedicated to

My grandmother Texie Cowell ~ I took back our voice! I'm

breaking the silence for us!

And to

my Pastor Michael D. Green Sr. ~ because of you I will continue to

become "My light is still on Green, Pops."

ACKNOWLEDGEMENTS

No book is written by just one person. Maybe these were my real-life experiences, but I wasn't alone. I'd like to extend some gratitude right through here!

To my friends and associates whom I've journeyed with along the way, both close and distant.

To my three siblings, Kentichia Taylor-Henderson, Kimberly Barnes, and Kennedy Cowell, for being consistent in my life no matter the circumstance.

To my oldest sister, more affectionately known as my sissy mom, for her consistent love, support, concern, correction, and prayers.

To my parents, Kennedy and Valerie Cowell, who remain relentless in this journey called life together. For the foundation of faith in God that they guided my siblings and I towards, and for showing their love, encouragement, and support when it matters most.

To my son for his many sacrifices. Thank you for your time, patience, love, humility, compassion, genuineness, courage, and much more. Thank you for being the treasured gift you are to me and so many, for growing with me through this process and journey. For the many days, nights, and random outbursts of prayer. I know there were times you thought your mom was crazy but, you never judged me. You encouraged me that I was great. I love you so much, son.

Most importantly, thank you, Yeshua Hamashiach, for allowing me to overcome, overtake and recover all. To live to share my journey that will change destiny, heal the heart, transform the mind, and ultimately save the life of every reader who will open their heart to this opportunity.

I love you, Lord.

Table of Contents

A NOTE FROM THE AUTHOR

 Welcome to your journey to experiencing healing, wholeness, and freedom.

I want to congratulate you because you have taken a step that many are not yet ready to take. You have chosen to take your life back from an abuser, which must be recognized.

Here is a hard truth. Sometimes you will feel alone, sometimes, you will feel a sense of peace that you cannot comprehend, and other times you will want to stop going through the steps in this book, but I need you to know that you are not alone.

Take your time. Allow yourself time to get to know the real you that has been in hiding while you were trying to make it in the world. Most importantly, include your Creator in every step so that your soul is reassured that you matter and are enough just because He created you.

It's Healing Time.

Let's Go.

Victoria Hardy

The Love Correction

12 Tools to Overcoming Trauma

The Love Correction

> *Anger is the language of the unheard.*

It is time for you to experience a life of true love, acceptance, hope, and healing. And the only way to make that happen is to learn what it means to love. Loving God, loving yourself, and loving others require something often destroyed through abuse and trauma. Trust.

The goal of this book is to guide you through trusting your voice, relying on God, applying wisdom when trusting people, and provoking you into the freedom of healing through transparency and accountability. Nothing in this world is more powerful than your story because it fuels your decisions. As we go on this journey together, you will learn the tools you need to overcome the trauma that has become a part of your story.

Your words have power. They have the power to heal and the power to kill. We will use your comments, and the Word of God, to break the authority that your experiences have wielded over your life.

If you have experienced trauma, you have got to get it out. Write it down as a story, create an album, paint, and write poems. Whatever you have to do, JUST GET IT OUT! Write the words so that the deep wounds they caused will no longer dominate your life.

Everyone will not understand what you are doing, and they might even try to discourage you, but I encourage you to permit yourself to be free.

When God put me on my healing journey, I had to face my abusers, acknowledge my acts of abuse and become an advocate for someone else who did not have a voice. I confronted my abuser and became an advocate for her and her daughter, who had been impregnated by her stepfather and punished by her mother for being raped. Her mother persuaded her to lie because she couldn't live without the man who had raped her daughter.

Sometimes the pain of what happens to you keeps you from trusting your voice, especially when the people supposed to protect and love you turn their back on you. I spoke up for my little cousin. I testified in court, told our family, and did everything I could to help her be safe. My family marginalized me, but I know that I did the right thing and it started me on the path to living my life outside the cycles that previously determined my decisions.

Older people would instruct me to stop telling so much of my story throughout my journey. I share my experiences, the good, the bad, and the ugly so that others can avoid some of the pitfalls and exploitation that followed me.

Now it is your turn to make a love correction and learn to trust again. You will find the wholeness you have longed for as you implement the tools in this book.

DISCLAIMER: The writings in this story will share intimate details regarding the abuse, injustice, uncertainty, and anguish I endured throughout my life. It is in no way an effort to diminish my family's values or my love for them. It is in no way an effort to expose or destroy the character of anyone included in my sharing my truth. If that were the case, I would not share my abusive actions and behaviors. I love everyone mentioned in this book with everything God has placed in me. It is also no reflection on their current state of life or being. It is time out for sweeping reality under the rug and expecting insanity to cease. It is time to do things differently to get a different result. My hope and intention are only to help set captives free and expose what so many of us harbor, not even realizing freedom is at our fingertips.

CHAPTER ONE
You Are Not Crazy

Covered wounds never heal

If you've ever been abused, you know the feeling of not being believed or validated. Abusers do this on purpose to make their victims feel like they are crazy and that what happened was not real. They may also try to convince the victim that it was their fault, or that nobody else would believe them. This is called gaslighting.

It is imperative to validate your experience and trauma. I know exactly how it feels to feel shame, hide from the past, and overcompensate or underachieve based on trauma, while questioning your recollection of what really happened.

Let me help you. You are not crazy. Yes, the abuse was actual; no, it was not your fault. You are not alone. You are now on the healing journey, and I am here to support you every step of the way.

Thank you for being brave enough to seek help.

What Is Abuse Anyway?

Have you ever wondered if what happened to you was abused?

I did.

You see, my family had a tradition of abuse. At six years old, my older cousin took me into a closet, with cold, brown cement walls and touched me. This time was the first of many secret excursions that my cousin and I took. As a matter of fact, when I became the older cousin, I continued this curse with 2 of my younger cousins, because that's just what was done. My young mind and body had been initiated into something that had implications that I could not even begin to understand at that age. That is why it is crucial that you know what abuse is, and how this violence can be applied to your soul.

Take a breath.

As you read the following definitions and descriptions, allow yourself to come to grips with the emotions, memories, and thoughts that may come flooding your mind, and know that you are not alone.

Abuse is any action that intentionally harms or injures another person. Abuse can be physical, psychological, emotional, sexual, or financial.

Types of Abuse Are:

- Physical abuse is any form of violence such as hitting, punching, slapping, grabbing, pushing, or kicking.

- Emotional abuse is any behavior that attacks your self-esteem or emotional stability.

- Psychological Abuse is a form of emotional abuse that involves using mind games to confuse, control, and manipulate you.

- Sexual abuse is any form of sexual contact or behavior that is unwanted or not consensual.

- Financial abuse is when someone takes control of your money or other possessions, prevents you from earning or managing your income or exploits you financially.

HEALING TIME:

It can be hard to know if you are being abused, incredibly emotionally or psychologically. Some common examples of abuse include being constantly criticized, being made to feel guilty or ashamed, being told that you're worthless or stupid, being ignored or dismissed, being isolated from friends and family, being ridiculed or degraded in front of others, or having your fears and concerns dismissed.

YOUR SPACE TO UNLOAD

____

____

____

____

____

____

____

____

____

YOUR SPACE TO UNLOAD

____

CHAPTER TWO

When It All Started

Leave no stone unturned, get it all out.

We may as well start from the beginning. I was born on August 1st, in the summer of 1986. My parents had already had two girls and one boy, so they anticipated the arrival of another boy, only to find out that I was a girl also. During my mother's pregnancy, she was in a brutal car accident that jeopardized both our lives and the life of my sister's Godmother who was driving.

When it had come time for my birth everyone was in for a great surprise. During those times, obstetrics were not as advanced as they are today, so once labor began, they discovered that I was coming out feet first. Being born breeched called for an emergency cesarean. My mother was cut from the belly button to the panty line, which reminded her constantly of my inconvenient birth. Not only was I, not the boy she so earnestly desired, but I also came out by my feet which were terrible, wrong, and nothing she anticipated.

There were 4 of us; my oldest sister, the submissive and obedient one, was favored and managed the house. She was the one who did everything my parents said and never disobeyed, and even when she became an adult it hurt her to break away. Even when my sister was 19 years old, she was still reprimanded for wanting to be human and do human things. I remember the only big fight she and my mom had where my mom pulled her by her hair almost to the ground.

After that my sister left home.

Next was my middle sister. She was always the rebellious one. She was the one who would fight with us all and scratch us up with her long nails. We visited our cousin's house a lot when we were younger; she would always play outside and disappear. My sister and older cousins would always leave me behind because they said that I would snitch on them. By the time I was in middle school, she was in high school and had met her high school sweetheart. They are still married with a beautiful family today. After my sister met him, she gave my mother HELL to be with her love. She would run away so much, and our mom put her in foster care.

There were countless fights. I remember the days and nights when my mother would cry and cry, and I would be the only one there to console and comfort her. We would both cry at times because I was hurting too. It had gotten to the point that everything revolved around my sister and her husband daily.

A man from our church also abused my sister. The church did nothing, and my father said we were no longer going back to that church. My mother, however, still serves loyally at this church today; although my father told us all those years ago to leave. This was an ongoing issue throughout our lives growing up and is still happening today.

Lastly, my brother was always a mix of my humble older sister and my rebellious middle sister. He was the only boy, and my mother ALWAYS favored him, while my father always placed a heavier expectation on him than he did on my sisters and I.

My brother goes to work, comes home, and only trusts animals and his girlfriend. He has no friends or social life and barely comes to family events. I am a hairstylist, so he always calls me to come over and do his hair, whether he had cornrows or the locs he has now (which is my specialty). One day I was doing his hair and even though I was terrified of my brother's quick temper, I had to ask him out loud, "Why did you bring me into your room at night and rub lotion on my breast? Why did you abuse me when we were home alone as we got older?"

He responded, "I don't know what you're talking about." After this, I realized that was all the closure I would get from him. There was no argument or fight and we just continued as we have been for years. I get to see my brother even though none of our family or childhood friends have seen him since he was maybe 19. He is an established welder and has been in this career since graduating high school. A lot of his bitterness and anger come from our upbringing. I totally understand why and do not hold any judgment about it.

After my sister was abused and my father stopped going to church, he pretty much submerged himself in working to provide for all of us, which he had always done alone and exceptionally. He started a business cleaning theater in Virginia and began to have my brother and his friends work with him in the family business. This stopped my brother from being forced to go to the Church that my mother refused to leave. He still resents my father for forcing him to work but never showing him how to love, and my mother for being passive-aggressive and narcissistic

Even today, my brother constantly rants about my father's infidelity, my mother's manipulation and control, and our toxic upbringing. Deep down inside I feel my brother has seen way more than he is willing to be transparent about, but no one can force him to share.

After my birth, it was apparent that my parents were not going to have any more children. My father worked vigorously to provide for a wife and four children. His time at home was very scarce; but every time my father would come home, he would spend a little more time with me than he did anyone else. He would do things like braid my hair, hold me, kiss me and care for me in ways that my other siblings did not receive. My father had unknowingly missed the opportunities to spend time with them. This is what I was told and too young to remember.

By the time I was 6 years old, I was introduced to what was being done in my family amongst the younger females. My cousin took me into a closet in the projects of Roberts Park. I still remember the brown, cold, cement walls and the holes that I could see in the metal stairs through the closet that she had taken me in that day. She touched me, and after that time it became what we all did together.

In my older life, I discovered that it was common for children to get curious and experiment with each other when there were no adults around, and that's just what we did. I thought I had continued this curse with a younger cousin. I was working towards my healing journey and had to go to that cousin and apologize, only to find out that she had already been touched by another cousin. It was then that I realized that generational curses and baggage attack an entire bloodline, not just one person. I discovered in this part of my journey that its intent was for bondage and baggage so that purpose and identity can never be initiated. You may never receive your breakthrough or have true freedom and healing without honesty and truth.

I remember that at about nine years old, I went over to a friend's house, and my mom finally allowed me to spend the night around the corner from my house. This was the first time I was ever touched by someone outside my family. This time it was one of my friend's boy cousins. The very next day I started my cycle, and my mother took me to CHKD hysterically. At that point I already had breasts, and the doctor assured my mother that girls were beginning their cycles sooner so there was no reason for her to be alarmed.

Admitting that you were abused, or allowing yourself to remember it, is sometimes challenging. But until you face the truth about your abuse, you cannot begin to overcome it.

As you take this journey with me, you will confront and face things that you would instead leave buried. You will begin to see how so many parts of your past were unmistakably marked by what happened to you with clarity. Then you will be empowered to break the hold of trauma, deep hurt, and wounds that have become a part of your story.

TOOL 1:

Acknowledge The Source and Where the Cycles Began

Learning to use this first tool was no easy feat. I had to sit down and consider the times when my soul and body were raped, terrorized, belittled, and undervalued and assess the damages.

"Whatever is has already been, and what will be has been before, and God will call the past to account." Ecclesiastes 3:15(NIV).

I spent my childhood trying to be enough so my parents would accept me; but no matter what I did or how I looked, I could never measure up.

As I went to the origin of each type of abuse I experienced, the cycles that were on repeat in my life became more apparent and I knew it was time to let it all go. I could not have done that without pinpointing where it all began.

Recounting all of the times I was devastated because my father only showed the affection and approval that I desperately craved to the women outside of our home uncovered the patterns that I accepted in relationships, and why I often tried to fix things by doing what I thought others wanted.

Sitting in the aftermath of being raped by men I trusted, living through narcissistic abuse, and suffering repeated rejection from my parents, husband, family, friends, and spiritual leaders opened my eyes. I began to understand why God initiated my healing journey in this way.

Acknowledging what happened and giving yourself space to see the domino effect it had on your life can be one of the greatest gifts you can provide to your future.

"Like a dog that returns to his vomit is a fool who repeats his foolishness." Proverbs 26:11(NIV)

You did not deserve what happened to you. It was not your fault. You did not choose to be abused, nor did you ask for it. The cycles triggered in your life do not originate with you, but they can stop with you.

Once I became aware of how the seeds of rejection and abuse planted, tilled, and harvested in my life had a chokehold on my growth and development, I could attack them head-on. I had to take ownership of every decision that I would make after my eyes were open and that was not easy.

Awareness gives you the strength and power to choose not to return to the circumstances, relationships, situations, and locations that trigger unhealthy cycles.

It will be hard and you must be committed to your future above all else. Prepare to be humiliated and disgusted, because you are not only going to re-visit what happened to you, the ugliest parts of who you are will be exposed.

TOOL 2:

Recognize You Need God, and in Most Cases Therapy

"Through pride and presumption come nothing but strife, but [skillful and godly] wisdom is with those who welcome [well-advised] counsel." - Proverbs 13:10 (AMP)

"Without consultation and wise advice, plans are frustrated, but with many counselors they are established and succeed." Proverbs 15:22

The [reverent] fear of the Lord [that is, worshiping Him and regarding Him as truly awesome] is the beginning and the preeminent part of knowledge [its starting point and its essence]; But arrogant fools despise [skillful and godly] wisdom and instruction and self-discipline." Proverbs 1:7(AMP)

Without an unbiased, knowledgeable resource we are left to our own devices which will very much lead us back to the place of trauma and harmful repetition. The most crucial counsel for us to seek is from our relationship with God and the development we experience through study, prayer, praise, and worship. This allows us to tap into the Holy Spirit, our Comforter and guide.

YOUR SPACE TO UNLOAD:

Before you reminisce, pray and ask God to guide you.

Father, I love you so much and I know you love me. I know this because throughout all I've seen and endured you've kept me here and I can take this journey to recovery. As I begin this journey, let your grace and love adhere to my mind. The things I may discover may not be favorable to me but out of the ashes, I will see your beauty in it all. Thank you for this opportunity to become all you've created me to be and be with me as we break down these walls and peel back the layers intended to keep me in captivity forever. Thank you for your liberty and freedom. In Jesus' Name, Amen

When you write, be thorough. Be gentle with yourself. Take breaks. Get someone to be with you. Do what you have to do, but don't give up.

YOUR SPACE TO UNLOAD

CHAPTER THREE

You Are Worthy

Is a dollar still a dollar, even after it has been compromised?
Your value can never depreciate!

When I was around nine years old, I attended Coleman Place Elementary in Norfolk, Virginia. And just like today, the kids were cruel. I was a little bit curvier, and like I said already had breasts. I would get humiliated and mocked all the time. For instance, when I would walk down the sidewalk after being released off the bus before school, the guys and girls would yell "EARTHQUUUUUAAAKKKEE" as if I were shaking the ground when I walked. Now, mind you, I wasn't the fattest girl of the bunch; but for some reason, it seemed ok to pick on me.

I remember getting close to one girl in particular and we would stay behind in class and hump on each other. I also remember there was one girl whom nobody would talk to and she would not speak to anyone else. She walked on the opposite side of the hallway away from other students. One day she broke her arm and struggled to get her coat on. Even though no one else would talk to her, I helped her put on her jacket. That one incident became something that she carried with her forever. We are friends until this day.

I found out in our adult life that she had severe anxiety and other mental issues because she was abused by a family member at a young age. It made her afraid of large crowds and required her to have a social distance to maintain her anxiety.

I left out this huge part where my mother and father were a part of the Apostolic Reformation which meant that we could only wear dresses or skirts - no pants, no tights, and no shorts. We were even required to wear head coverings to church. Not only was I picked on for being heavier, I always had to wear skirts. That was a complete joke. By the time I got to fifth grade, my mother had slightly given in and allowed us to start to wear pants, but we had to shop in the men's section. I would wear Bugle Boy pants from Burlington Coat Factory, Etonics, Fila, and brands of that nature so everything was baggy and boyish. I assume this was to hide my figure or something. I still do not know why she made us wear men's clothes.

Once I got to middle school, I thought that things began to evolve and get better. I started to make friends. I was a little more stylish since I could wear pants. Then one day a girl that I really admired, whom I will leave unnamed, looked at me and told me that she did not want me around her or to be my friend. I thought we mutually cared for one another, but that day I learned that it was one-sided. Shortly after that, I met two friends and we became the 3 Ps. They had their Hispanic culture in common, but I was included because we all just loved each other. As time went on, we all kind of started to make other friends, and I wanted to be friends with everybody. It came to a point where I was made to choose. I didn't want to choose. I wanted to be friends with everyone, whether they liked each other or not, I loved them all. This became a significant problem and eventually put me on the outside of everyone once again.

Rejection, isolation, abandonment, and a sense of not belonging seemed to follow me.

I ALWAYS loved music, so I connected with some other friends and we had fun together. We thought we were Destiny's Child and even competed in the talent show at Azalea Gardens Middle School! While I was in middle school in the 6th grade, I met Richard. Richard was my brother's girlfriend's brother and was between 17 and 18 years old even though he was in middle school. He was a white boy who talked and acted like us - if you know what I mean.

I fell in love with Richard, or at least I thought I did. We would write each other long love letters full of the promises we had made to one another. We would find a way to hang out and spend time together. This was the first person and the first time I willingly had sex. One day, I decided to do something I had never done before. I would skip school to be with Richard, who was fearless and drank and smoked. The only people that I told were the Ps. I told them my entire plan. When I returned to school expecting to just get on the bus and go home, my parents were waiting for me. My father worked from sunup to sundown, but when it was time to discipline, humiliate, triangulate or devalue us, my mother would ensure he was involved.

I remember I had a Greek principal and my father worked at a Greek restaurant. After my father dumped my book bag and discovered all the letters Richard and I had written to each other, he was furious. My principal excused herself and told my dad to do whatever he needed. He then whipped me in the principal's office, and I was suspended for a week. They pressed charges against Richard. Once that was all over, due to some sort of mental issue his mother fought for, he was able to maintain his freedom. I had hoped he would be free because Richard gave me the time and words I needed from my father. Although our ages were drastically different, he was kind and respectful. We cared about each other, as he had come from a toxic home as well. We were trauma-bonded, but at that age, it was love.

After this, promiscuity became how I filled the void for the love I wasn't receiving at home. Of course, I didn't realize that then. All of my relationships began to overlap and I was never just talking or dealing with one boy at a time. I actually thought these guys and my so-called friends cared about me when in fact they were laughing at me and talking about me behind my back.

Once I got to high school, I had my first open same-sex relationship and also started to date the person who would end up being my husband when I turned 18 years old. High School was not better than any of the years before. I had made a reputation for myself at that point and didn't fit in with any class of people. Either I was the church girl who was different or the hoe who wanted everybody's man. This was not true, but it was how I was perceived.

I had associates and friends of course, but there were two of my male friends, whom I would look forward to being with every day for protection. They treated me like I was one of the guys. I would meet them every day by the lunchroom doors so we could hang out until classes started and no one would bother me.

But after school things were different. On one occasion, a group of neighborhood girls, pretending to be my friends, lured me to the end of my neighborhood block and all began assaulting me at once. We used to call that "getting banked." It is funny now, but then I was so confused and embarrassed. There was another time I remember getting off the bus like any other day. I had no idea that it had been the talk of the school the whole day that this one girl and the ENTIRE neighborhood and school were following me home to fight. The only thing I was thinking once I realized what was happening was, "Lord, please let me get to my house so at least this time I won't be fighting alone." My siblings and mom would be home and let me fight this girl alone. It is so funny now, but not that day.

I felt isolated, abandoned, misunderstood, ashamed, and rejected. I had known the girl since elementary school. We had never argued or exchanged any words. Here we are now in high school and out of nowhere, she brought the entire neighborhood to watch us fight. Until this day, the only reason I can think of is that she assumed that I was or wanted to be in a relationship with a boy that she was seeing at the time. In fact, his cousin became my brother-in-law about a year after this incident, because he was dating my sister. Little did she or anyone know, we were all like family.

Everything I experienced up to that point played into the cycle of trauma that had begun when I was born. Little did I know that I would meet my future husband around 13 after my father left the church. At this time, I had begun traveling with my oldest sister. I affectionately refer to her as my Sissymom, because I've always admired her integrity, poise, character and so many things. I often slept in her bed. She would let me rub her ears until I fell asleep until I got too old to be doing it. Anyway, I started going to church with her sometimes. She was dating her future husband, an evangelist who is now deceased, and I would travel with them to the revivals he would preach. That is when I met my ex-husband.

He was 14 years old and was already a minister. When he saw me, he and his friend made a bet about who would talk to me first. He pulled up on me in this blue Hawaiian shirt, which was the style then, and swept me off my feet with how kind and respectful he was. I would sneak and call him, and he would say he couldn't talk because he had to do chores, study, or go to church. He was so different. All the other boys would agree to sneak and creep all through the night, but until we got a little older he would never do that.

We dated off and on throughout high school, and I would go between him and another guy I thought I wanted from my church. This boy was the first guy to ever speak a word-curse over me. He said no man would ever want me for anything but my bottom. Of course, he didn't say it that way. He was a few years ahead of me and went to a different school. My parents still didn't allow me to date, so I could not go to his prom with him. He trashed me and went with the other girl he was dating at his school. I think he also found out that I was talking to a guy who attended the alternative school where he worked. He later married, had children, and divorced that girl.

Tool 3
Realize You Are Worth it and Worthy. No Matter What Has Happened, You Still Have Value

"Are not five sparrows sold for two [a]copper coins? Yet not one of them has [ever] been forgotten in the presence of God. 7 Indeed the very hairs of your head are all numbered. Do not be afraid; you are far more valuable than many sparrows." Luke 12:6-7(AMP)

"The Lord your God is in your midst, A Warrior who saves. He will rejoice over you with joy; He will be quiet in His love [making no mention of your past sins], He will rejoice over you with shouts of joy." Zephaniah 3:17(AMP)

And I will also make a nation of [Ishmael] the son of the maid because he is your descendant." Genesis 21:13

There were many times in my life when I was made to feel unworthy. The first time was when my father, who was upset about my promiscuity told me, "I'll tell you what. Your looks only gone take you but so far." But then we would see Mariah Carey on television, and he would repeat repeatedly, "That's a beautiful woman. She's just as beautiful as she wanna be." His words and actions told me that I was not valuable enough.

Fast forward to my senior year in high school, my mother left me alone to live with my dad and as the baby, of course, I was home alone. I was between dating my future husband and a friend who became more at the time when the home that I had lived in since I was five years old caught fire. It was around Christmas, so all of my Christmas gifts were destroyed. Our church at the time barely gathered a few hundred dollars to help us. Thankfully my dad was a fantastic steward over money, his family, and our home. He had homeowner's insurance, so we were able to recover.

Here I am a senior in high school who went from being the baby in the home to the only child. Although my father had excellent insurance, I went from sleeping in my own home to sleeping in the projects with my aunt with roaches crawling at night and constant disturbance while our home was being repaired. That great friend whom I dated would pick me up for school and be there for me. My ex-husband's family tried to assist us and even allowed me to stay with them for a few nights, even though they were pastors.

When it had come close to the time for my mom to return from Germany, where she was helping my sister with her second child, my dad finally took me to this beautiful fully furnished apartment where the local news reporter lived. They had a maid and everything. In hindsight, I realized that while I was sleeping in the bed with my auntie, with roaches crawling every night and gunshots raving, my father was sleeping in a penthouse suite with maid service for about six months.

I was so happy to be there. I'd return to the apartment to find that the clothes I had left on the floor would be neatly folded on my bed, or the dishes from breakfast would be mysteriously cleaned. I still do not understand until this day why my dad was content with letting me stay with my aunt while he lived lavishly for all that time. Maybe he just needed peace or to be alone. I am not sure. But that was one of the hardest times of my teenage years, and I needed him to be there for me and show me that I was worth it. Instead, he showed me that in the hardest of times, I was the least priority.

The guy who told me the only reason that anyone would want me was because my rear end made me feel so worthless. I started to make my personality small so that I did not bring attention to myself. I did not look in the mirror, because I hated myself and felt devalued, ugly, and unworthy. I could not change my body so instead, I dumbed myself down in hopes that no one would see me at all.

One day I saw a demonstration done by Tye Tribbet. He asked a young woman to come from the audience. Then he took a twenty-dollar bill out of his pocket, crumpled it up, stumped on it, and almost destroyed it, but when he asked her if she still wanted the money, she said, "Absolutely!"

The point of this demonstration was to show that your value does not depreciate because something terrible has happened to you. You become more valuable because you endured and have come out on the other side. Even if you feel at the bottom, you are still here. You did not commit suicide.

Sickness did not take over your body. You are still here to walk out the purpose God has prepared for you.

YOUR SPACE TO UNLOAD

CHAPTER FOUR

Time to Detox

> **"**
>
> *Empty your cup so God can fill you up*

Of course, at 18 years old, I got married. On the morning of Thanksgiving or Christmas after my graduation, my ex-husband proposed to me in the kitchen in front of his mother.

His mother was on the phone, and exclaimed, "Oh my God! This boy is not! Don't do it!"

Even though she was right, at that moment my proposal was ruined. Who wants to hear their future mother-in-law, whom they loved like a mother, tell her son not to marry her? I could not believe it, because we had never had trouble or anything. I respected her more than my mom at the time because she was there for me and supported me in ways my mother had never done in my entire life. She knew something we did not though.

My ex-husband and I argued until the week we got married and even made a vow that if we could not get it right before the New Year we would call off the wedding. Our pride would not allow us to do that. Everybody had already anticipated the wedding, and so did we. We had planned this since we were kids. So we married and vowed to each other that ministry would begin at home and we would not be the statistically young marriage that ended in divorce.

For years we fought, separated, and fought. I cheated. We lived with family members. We fought. We spoiled each other our entire marriage and we fought. He drowned himself in ministry and I cheated some more. It was a never-ending cycle because we were both so full of childhood trauma, pain from the past, and the secrets we withheld from each other. There was no way we could ever see eye to eye. The generational curses from him and me created the perfect combination for the enemy. His inability to show affection and my need for validation made the perfect recipe for the enemy to make a spectacle of God's intention for covenant.

I remember one day sitting in church with my husband, not feeling so well, and I leaned my head against his arm.

He shook me off and said "What are you doing? We're in church!"

As if public displays of affection were disgusting. My ex-husband would have dreams when I was involved with someone behind his back. He would be so bitter all the time, and instead of ministry beginning at home bitterness set in. Every time I had to prepare for youth revivals, I knew that I would have to stand at the altar and watch him pray for the deliverance of a young woman, who was molested, abused, struggling, or had a dirty past just like me, while he couldn't see my pain and pray me through. I found myself in the arms of someone else for that love, just as I did from my father's wounds.

I remember we both wanted a child so badly. We prayed and I cried. I would even do exercises after intercourse to try and get that baby in my belly. We ended up separating for the last time after going home and living with his parents for about six months. I moved out and got a place of my own.

I was dating a much older woman this time around. But this evening, I remember standing in the Kappital Cuts parking lot where my ex-husband introduced me to one of his new friends and suggested that we link up. Well, we did and began having sex maybe a month later. I was working for Wachovia then. This guy would take my car every day while I was at work and pick me up with a full tank of gas. We kept on for a few months, and it fizzled out because I later learned he had gotten married.

I had forgotten all about wanting a baby. All I wanted at this point was my marriage back because this guy had worn me out like a rag with the drama and scandals in the short time, we were together. A few weeks later, after my husband and I reconciled, we had sex and he immediately said,

"YOU'RE PREGNANT!"

I denied it because at that point I knew two things. One, my body was as curvy as it had ever been and my skin was glowing. And two, if I were pregnant, it would be a close call that he was not the father. I took so many Dollar Tree pregnancy tests until I had to confirm for myself finally. I went to the emergency room and saw on an ultrasound that I was indeed six weeks and two days pregnant. The only way that he could have known this was if God had told him.

I scheduled an abortion because I did not want to take a chance and have my son's legacy be like his biological father's. I remember it was Friday the 13th and I said, "God please help me."

I was substituting at the Wachovia near the Courthouse on Cedar Road, and God showed me the day my son was conceived and said to me, "This child has a purpose."

I immediately went to the bathroom at Wachovia and told my husband that I was pregnant and everyone was happy.

"Is there a chance he isn't mine?"

My ex-husband asked me two times before we were finally divorced, once before my son was born and the last time when he was two years old.

I was honest with him and said, "Yes, of course, there is. We were separated."

It wasn't until my son turned seven that he decided to get a paternity test. It came back with a 0% probability that my husband was the father. This shook our world but gave me peace. I had endured years of emotional, verbal, and psychological abuse from my ex-husband because I felt I deserved it. After that, something unlocked in me to fight for myself a little more.

My son's biological father claimed to want a family at that time, but in reality, he was just homeless again and needed a place to live. When I stood my ground, he moved across the street to my neighbor who dated him right in my face. When I found out, I kindly traveled his bags across the court of our projects and told her the truth about who he was to my son and me.

Tool 4: Detox old habits that are oppressing and recognize the role you play in your cycles of trauma and abuse.

"If we confess our sins, he is faithful and just to forgive us our sins and to cleanse us from all unrighteousness." 1 John 1:9 (NIV)

"Turn away from evil and do good; seek peace and pursue it."
Psalm 34:14 (NIV)

I had to be honest and look at habits that were causing oppression in my life. If what I was doing did not lead to a state of mind that allowed me to live in my purpose, I had to stop it.

Learning to get out of the negative thoughts and away from negative people, refusing to engage in negative actions, and being intentional about forcing positive, life-giving words into my mind helped me to get to the place of healing that I have today. Negativity is no longer the normal state of affairs in my thoughts.

This is almost the most crucial step because true repentance and transformation can only occur when there is responsibility and accountability. Running away from issues won't fix them. You have to address them head-on. Often, you will continue to have the same cycles and tests until you have learned the necessary lessons for your progression. Romans 7:25 says that we serve God with our minds, but we serve sin with our flesh. Through this, I understand that my cycles may occur in response to my desires when I don't submit them to God and renew my mind.

YOUR SPACE TO UNLOAD

CHAPTER FIVE

Find Your Focus

"

Enough has got to be enough

I was in this last relationship behind my husband's back and the guy ended up sleeping with my sister-in-law. We set him up to be caught as if I was not married to someone else. How ironic. In hindsight, I think my sister-in-law might have been trying to hurt me for hurting her brother. She even hooked me up with one of her friends and had him take nude photos of me that he would use to humiliate and threaten me. On another occasion, she turned down one of her married friends, who was a cheater, and told him to take a chance with me.

I wanted to be a part of something so bad, that I would do anything, even if it were horrible. At least I was considered family. My ex warned me, in his own way. Later he admitted that he wanted to protect me from his family but I would not listen. I thought he was just trying to control me and have me all to himself to ignore and sexualize. That may not have been his intention, but that is how his actions made me feel.

For instance, the dating stopped but he never stopped wanting to have sex. Even after our son was born, there were days that he would walk into the house and scream that he did not want to be bothered and needed time alone. So I kept our son upstairs, quietly watching Tye Tribbett and beating his drums. Meanwhile, I would hear him on the phone with his God-brother, who was also a preacher. They would spend hours and late nights on the phone talking about I don't know what, then he would try for sex in the wee hours of the morning. Sometimes we went months without intimacy, for so many reason, and at the fault of us both.

Toward the end where I felt the urgency to confess my infidelity. I remember we went to a concert at the Pavilion in Portsmouth, and I heard a man's testimony of how he revealed his cheating to his wife after God had been dealing with him about it heavily. He went on to say that he and his wife survived and were thriving.

About 2 months later, I remember it was one Sunday after church and I could no longer bear living another day bound by the lies and manipulation it took to maintain myself. I wanted to be free from the monster I had become so I stood in his face and confessed every lie and cheat. Afterward, I let him ask every question he wanted, and no matter how devastating it felt, I answered honestly.

He looked at me immediately and said, "And now you're the woman I want. Even more now I know you won't lie to me. I want to make this work."

Not long after that, I met my first test and I failed again. I realized I was just too broken and could not stand to go back to lying and being unhappy, so I said, "Let's end it." Little did I know, I was walking right into disobedience and into reaping what I had sown. This was the beginning of my narcissistic abuse cycle.

I went back home to live with my parents who were nesting. I was dealing with a gentleman at the time who had told me we were best friends. He claimed that he felt so guilty about being with me because he felt that he was the reason my marriage ended. We fought and he took me around his friends. He told me things in private and then treated me differently around these certain people. He always said to me about his insecurities and I was always there to encourage him. Once it got closer to the time that he was done with me and I had served my purpose, the more he began to devalue me.

I recall him using his mother to triangulate me. She told me that I was a little domineering. This is how he wanted everyone to see me. There was a certain group of people whom he always wanted to receive acceptance from, and they would always make him feel rejected and unwanted. I was there to uplift him each time he felt rejected. All the while, he was using me so that they would include him. He soon began dating someone else in this group and abandoned me.

I remember the day I finally realized my place and stopped chasing him. On this day, he double-booked time with both me and the new girl (whom he later married) and forgot to end the call with me. I heard him telling her horrible things about me and why he hated me so much. We all became friends, and for years he still treated me like the second woman, and his wife for whatever reason had no issue with it. In this group of people, all of the musicians had a wife and a side piece. That is the label they wanted me to uphold, but I refused. For many years I allowed our friendship to continue and the soul tie was strong. It seemed like every time I would be in distress or in a bad relationship that ended in shame, he and his wife would reappear and be right there – a soul tie.

Tool 5: Stop pleasing people and seek to please God.

"Rendering service with goodwill, as to the Lord, and not [only] to men," Ephesians 6:7(AMP)

"Whatever you do, work from the soul, as [something done] for the Lord and not for men," Colossians 3:23 (AMP)

"It is better to take refuge in the Lord than to trust in man." Psalm 118:8(NIV)

"But just as we have been approved by God to be entrusted with the gospel, so we speak, not to please man, but to please God who tests our hearts." 1Thessalonians 2:4 (NIV)

"The fear of man lays a snare, but whoever trusts in the Lord is safe." Proverbs 29:25 (NIV)

"For am I now seeking the approval of man, or God? Or am I trying to please man? If I were still trying to please man, I would not be a servant of Christ." Galatians 1:10(NIV)

As a survivor of narcissistic abuse, I can tell you that it makes you want to live for others. You live your life worrying about what other people like you to do so that eventually, you do not know what you want anymore.

I wanted so badly to receive love and acceptance from my mom that I followed her passion and purpose. I tried to make her happy, make her love me, and most of all, make her see me. Living this way caused me to dim my light.

I was so focused on making everyone happy that I was willing to throw away my sense of security and belonging to please others. That is why I had to consume my life with God and His will for my life to keep my soul full.

This mindset is crippling. Finding fulfillment in the validation of others will always give them the barometer for your success. The minute they discount or disregard you is the moment that you lose yourself all over again. It cripples you, keeping you from acknowledging the wonderful investment that God made in you to share with others because your lens is so clouded with opinions that should not matter. This has to end so that you can discover your truth and life can begin.

YOUR SPACE TO UNLOAD

CHAPTER SIX

Pursue Your Purpose

I cried for help, but no one heard me. My wounds were exposed, but no one saw me. Who will cry for the little girl?

My cousin who first abused me in the closet of her family's home ended up on trial for events like "The Precious Story". If you saw the movie, "Precious" then I do not have to explain further. My cousin's husband impregnated her daughter. I was going to advocate for this baby because everyone else in my family wanted to cover it up.

So I went to the courthouse intending to tell someone, ANYONE, that my cousin was not well and this was all a tragedy. Well, when I got to the courthouse, my cousin and I were getting out of the car at the same time. I felt like, "this is my moment," so I looked over at her and said,

"You know, what happened in that closet when I was 6 years old, changed my life forever and I've struggled ever since."

She said, "Ok" and that was it. I remember reminding her that she knew what was happening with her daughter. "After she told you she had been touched at 6 or 7, you cried to her about the man leaving you all. She loved you so much she lied for you and felt responsible for him."

She replied by saying something like, "she was being grown and nobody told her to feel responsible." From that point, I did not speak to her anymore because it was clear that in her mind she was right and decent and good. She blamed her daughter for everything, just like in the movie, "Precious." She tried to convince the judges that her daughter was "fast" and "out of control" when she was the most submissive person, especially to her mother.

After I advocated for my young cousin, my family pretty much blackballed me. They ceased all communication with me. My mother kept asking me why I would help this cause and told me not to embarrass the family. I kept advocating and telling my mom that this is why the curse continues. There can be no healing where there is no exposure. She and her side of the family were angry with me, especially after my cousin was convicted and sent to prison

It was not because of me. But maybe if I had not told the counselor about our childhood, and my cousin's illness, and asked them to stop what was happening, that baby might have had more children by another man. It was not going to stop.

My cousin had no remorse and still cries for empathy.

My mom says I don't know her side of the story, but I do. Hurting people hurt people; however, just like I have taken responsibility and my life back after the abuse, we all have a choice. It does not matter if we cannot help it, we should find a way to not terrorize others. Even if that means being like my brother and never seeing people because it is better than causing more harm in the world

Tool 6: Find fulfillment in your God-given purpose.

"I cry out to God Most High, to God who fulfills his purpose for me"
Psalm 57:2 (NIV)

"Many are the plans in the mind of a man, but it is the purpose of the Lord that will stand." Proverbs 19:21 (NIV)

"For we are his workmanship, created in Christ Jesus for good works, which God prepared beforehand, that we should walk in them" Ephesians 2:10 (KJV)

"And we know that for those who love God all things work together for good, for those who are called according to his purpose." Romans 8:28 (KJV)

I found fulfillment when I advocated for my cousin. I hate injustice and I refuse to stand by and allow someone to be abused without doing something about it in my power. I have always dreamed and desired to be a light for Christ. I am passionate about empowering young women, so when I met a young woman, whom I never anticipated would be my cousin's wife one day, who submitted to me for guidance I knew I was on the right track. One day she told me, "People always focus on young women, but the men are often forgotten." After that, the next generation altogether became a burden on my heart. Realizing that my son is a part of the future generation changed my posture. Instead of just advocating for the mental, emotional, and physical health of young women, I now also advocate for the young men who will become our next leaders to empower them to take back the role of authority and dominion that God gave to Adam over the earth.

I lived the first part of my thirties searching, hoping, and praying for a mentor. I thought I needed someone to build a model for myself and my purpose and destiny. I began to idolize that idea and again God showed me that He is and will always be my ultimate source.

He gave me a new name, and a fresh perspective, and established my identity, purpose, and value. He showed me that after all that I had endured and survived, He wouldn't allow His Glory to be shared with any human being. His plans for me were supernatural and only He could do it. Only He could make me whole. Only He could fill every void. Only He could validate me.

YOUR SPACE TO UNLOAD

____

____

____

____

____

____

____

____

____

____

____

____

CHAPTER SEVEN

Get Filled Up

> *Thanksgiving is the key to the door of purpose*

After my divorce, I slowed down a lot, but I still had such a longing for love, intimacy, and belonging. I found a new church home and started my first real relationship after being divorced. A soul tie was formed. He was the drummer at the time and was the first man that ever told me that God said I was his wife.

I was bitter and broken from my previous experience, after my marriage, of being used for acceptance. Although I felt the same about him, I allowed my past to tear us apart. I was ashamed that we were intimate before being married, and I had questions about his sexuality because of his friends. We ended up having a messy breakup before our pastor was incarcerated.

Still wounded and operating under curses, we went to a service in Suffolk where a man who was a pastor spotted and approached me. My current pastor at the time, my Godfather, and my Godmother all warned me that this man was dangerous and was not good for me. In 2011, I soon found out how true this was.

I had taken my first vow of celibacy and told him I was waiting until marriage to have sex and that I had finally gotten approved for low-income housing. This pastor and my ex-husband helped me move into my new apartment in Calvert Square.

Even though I had told him about my vow he would still make advances. One day we were fighting and I told him I wanted to break things off a bit and slow down. A few weeks later, he asked me to come to Suffolk and help him move from his apartment into a new place. He had been having some hardships and I was so excited that things were turning around for him, that I enthusiastically said yes.

When I got to his apartment, there was no power. The apartment seemed empty, but it was dirty with a bit of rubbish and debris scattered around. He immediately began antagonizing me about my vow saying, "There's no way no one's getting it." He pushed me into the closet of that filthy apartment and assaulted me. Exhausted from screaming and fighting, I fell to the floor crying after he was done.

He walked into the restroom and came back with a used roll of toilet paper, threw it at me, and said, "I just had to make sure. Now clean yourself up."

After more crying, arguing, and manipulation, we traveled back to Norfolk and I found out that he had gotten a room in a halfway house that was just miles away from me in the Park Place area. He visited me frequently and claimed that he would now respect my vow. He had tested me and felt that I was honest and not sleeping around.

My desire to be validated loved and accepted put me in very dangerous spaces. I just wanted someone to see me, value me, and affirm me, but I now know that I only needed this from God. After a while, his abuse became consistent. It was like he transformed into a different person whenever he came to my apartment.

One day he said to me, "Give it to me or you know I'll take it."

I did not even have my bed yet, so that he would assault me on the bottom bunk in my son's room. It had gotten so bad, that I knew I had to get away. I did not doubt in my mind that he would end up physically abusing or even killing me if things kept going in the same direction.

I was sitting in the car with one of my friends and he drove up to us. He got out of his car and approached us, telling my friend,

"Tell her to get out of your car, or I'll beat you and her."

As he began to walk up to the car and grabbed for my door handle, I screamed, "DRIIIIIVE!"

When I arrived home, he was in the shower so I called the police. That day the officers told me he was wanted in another neighborhood close to mine and took him away. That was the last day I saw him in person, but he haunted me for years.

I would often dream of him sitting on my bed, waiting for me when I got home at night with that wicked smile on his face.

As if being tormented in my dreams wasn't enough, he would find a way to contact me. It seemed he got a kick out of blocking and unblocking me on Facebook to send me messages about his amazing life.

Tool 7: Pray and consistently fill your heart and mind with scripture and healthy knowledge. Empower yourself through affirmations, self-help literature, music, and motivational videos.

"If my people who are called by my name humble themselves, and pray and seek my face and turn from their wicked ways, then I will hear from heaven and will forgive their sin and heal their land." 2 Chronicles 7:14

"You will make your prayer to him, and he will hear you, and you will pay your vows." Job 22:27

"Is anyone among you suffering? Let him pray. Is anyone cheerful? Let him sing praise." James 5:13

This part of the process required me to recondition myself. I had to correct thoughts that brought defeat into my life. I make sure that I am consistently feeding my mind things that produce faith and positivity so that my default is to respond to circumstances healthily, instead of falling into old patterns of thought and behavior that only bring me pain and calamity.

Increase your prayer and devotion time slowly. It is okay to set a prayer schedule so that you can build your soul and get used to living a life full of the Spirit.

Make sure that you feed your subconscious mind with faith and positivity. Fall asleep with something that feeds your soul to develop a mindset of peace and hope.

Having a heart of gratitude is an important step in empowering yourself. The more that you thank God, the more He will show and guide you into whom you were created to be and lead you to your purpose.

Remember that when you use this tool, you will build endurance and increase what you receive through the amount and frequency you determine to fill yourself up with the foundation you need to keep healing. It may not happen overnight, so it is crucial that you extend grace to yourself for errors.

YOUR SPACE TO UNLOAD

CHAPTER EIGHT
Pull The Trigger

My validation was in his infatuation, them father wounds run deep

I remembered when I wanted and needed to hear my father say, "You're beautiful and I love you," or "You're talented, gifted, and will be successful." Instead, my memory is stained with the times that my mom, sisters, and I had to watch my dad compliment and kiss other women in church on the cheek, and then listen to him tell us how beautiful these women were afterward when we yearned for him to treat us in the same manner. To be honest, I will not speak for them, but I know I need it. Every daughter deserves to be validated and affirmed.

I will never forget the day my father almost drove us into oncoming traffic because he was bottlenecking to watch a beautiful, curvy woman walk down the street. That recollection is imprinted in my memory like a movie.

Until this day, it triggers me if I am in a relationship with a man who has a wandering eye. It is something that I cannot stand. After all, I grew up watching my father give the validation I needed to other women, even to the point where he put my life in danger because he could not help himself.

The only time I remember my father talking about my appearance was when he told me disapprovingly that my looks would only take me so far. That created a sense of discomfort in me about how I look. I don't want any attention on my physical appearance. As a matter of fact, that is still a trigger for me today. If someone constantly comments on my physical appearance, it makes me uncomfortable because I don't want that to be the focus of my platonic relationships.

On my healing journey, I have had to pay attention to what triggers me and causes me to go back to the place I was traumatized so that I could begin to heal more and deal with the reasons behind the triggers.

Tool 8: Experiencing any type of trauma leaves you with triggers. Identify your triggers.

"You were running well. Who hindered you from obeying the truth?" Galatians 5:7 (NIV)

"Whoever conceals his transgressions will not prosper, but he who confesses and forsakes them will obtain mercy." Proverbs 28:13 (NIV)

This tool requires brutal honesty. You have to be honest about your triggers with yourself and with those around you. This helps to keep you safe and to build genuine relationships.

Once you have figured out what triggers you, redirect your heart so that your interactions are not trauma responses, but genuine connections.

I have learned not to withdraw when I am triggered. I pay attention, but those things do not control me. I have learned to trust my voice so that I can distinguish if the emotions and warning signals that the trigger has activated are based in fact or are founded in fear of what has happened to me in the past.

I now realize that from the time I was born, the enemy was out for my identity, my voice, my light, and my purpose. My purpose was disguised in narcissistic abuse, manipulation, and the need for validation. God has given me confidence in Him that needs no fleshly affirmation.

YOUR SPACE TO UNLOAD

CHAPTER NINE

Plan Your Way Out

Refuse to become what hurt you! Fight for your freedom!

Tool 9: Create realistic alternatives to apply when triggers are encountered.

In the past, I had a cycle of resorting to adding marijuana when I was triggered into depression. It seemed like every season, things would go the same, and someone with the same issues and addictions would magically appear. This was no magic. It was spiritual, and I had to break the covenant with depression and addiction in my bloodline, just like I had with abuse, molestation, and the need for validation.

For years, I had to repeat many tests until I learned to be honest about my triggers, boundaries, wants, and needs. I remember when I bought my first house. My mother was helping me to get some things in order, but we got into a bit of a conflict.

In response to our disagreement, she said, "I'm forcing myself to be happy for you as it is."

This was nothing new in the interactions that I had with my mother since childhood. I spent so much time trying to please her and gain her approval that I even chose my career in an attempt to make her proud of me. But nothing I did was ever good enough.

Because of instances like these that defined my life, I always feared that I would become a narcissistic mother with my son. I constantly war with that thought and am transparent with my son about everything. We attend counseling periodically and maintain an open relationship. When I am wrong, my son uses his voice to tell me, and I make a conscious effort to understand him and change the toxic parenting behaviors I learned growing up.

Many times, my son does not even have to bring anything to me, because when I recognize what happened, I show him and then apologize.

I had to make a pathway for my healing by creating a way to deal with triggers when I encounter them.

"Finally, brothers, whatever is true, whatever is honorable, whatever is just, whatever is pure, whatever is lovely, whatever is commendable, if there is any excellence, if there is anything worthy of praise, think about these things. What you have learned and received and heard and seen in me—practice these things, and the God of peace will be with you." Philippians 4:8-9(NIV)

"Humble yourselves, therefore, under the mighty hand of God so that at the proper time he may exalt you, casting all your anxieties on him, because he cares for you." 1 Peter 5:6-7(ESV)

It is important that you plan your way of escape so that you do not fall back into old habits. If you do not know what triggers you, then you cannot address them and start to make different choices.

Create a practical plan that will help you counteract old behavior patterns when triggered. For example, instead of withdrawing, allow yourself to be open with the safe people that are around you, or instead of doing something that you would regret, have a list of activities that you will engage in to keep yourself on the path to healing.

YOUR SPACE TO UNLOAD

CHAPTER TEN

Release the Shame

Don't wear your past like a second skin, it didn't defeat you!

Throughout my adult life, I have found myself drawn to women like my mother. These women wanted to be idolized, adored, and served. I was a beautiful girl with low self-worth, a need for validation, and low esteem, searching for a place to belong. I was exactly what they were looking for. These women in power and high positions did one of two things. They rejected me which made me put them on a pedestal and idolize them. I would think, wow, how did you become so great that you can choose whom you accept, love or validate from God's children. Or they would seek me out, hoping to make and mold me into a mini version of them or what they wanted me to be. Because of my parenting wounds and low self-esteem, I felt blessed that they chose to mentor me and allow me to be connected to them. I thought it was such an honor.

During these times, I would submit myself to them to be accepted for who I was. I began to realize that those ladies were struggling with the same things that I was fighting, low self-esteem, wounds of trauma and narcissistic abuse, and wounds from their parents. Then I woke up and started to learn my worth.

I recognized that not only did my mentors have self-esteem issues, but they also needed me because of what I stood for and had to offer. Instead of being transparent and embracing an exchange, they pursued submission through oppressive implications. Religiosity had taught them that false humility and oppression meant Godly submission and humility.

Even amid my healing and seeking acceptance, I had no problem separating myself from anything if it affected my wholeness. They would stay connected to toxic environments for status and did not dare to leave and rebuild. I did not care about my situation. My concern was and always will be my wholeness and operating in the right state of mind so that God is pleased.

I always ended up in relationships with these dynamics, because I just wanted someone to see me as great and affirm me. These connections never failed in leaving me feeling empty inside. Those women could not fill my desire for what I felt I was missing from my mother. The truth is that they were looking for their source of fulfillment in me.

Only the Creator and self-awareness could make me feel complete. I am so grateful that I have learned what triggers me and how to identify when these types of relationships are presented to me so that I can protect my peace and healing journey.

This has only been made possible because I am doing the work that goes along with submitting to God. My freedom depends on my cooperation with the principles and tools that He has given me to walk in victory.

Tool 10: Refuse to go in unhealthy spaces and environments by becoming aware of your weakness and distractions and avoiding them.

"Submit yourselves therefore to God. Resist the devil, and he will flee from you." James 4:7 (KJV)

Be very careful in recognizing the cycles of abuse. When you become aware, get out. Follow your discernment at all times. This is why you need to know your triggers so you do not put yourself in situations where you will return to a place of pain.

The rejection from a mother will cause you to idolize women because of your desire for true love and acceptance that you never received from your mom. Rejection of all kinds breeds idolatry; and as I look back over my journey, I can see now that I was struggling with idolatry. During those years when I was trying to get approval from others, I gave them the adoration that only belongs to God; therefore, they had become idols.

In my earlier years, all of the love, affirmation, and affection that I sought from men was made to fulfill the longing for the love, affection, attention, and validation of my father. When I finally shared my abuse with my dad, it gave me strength and brought us closer. He began to understand why I did what I had done and even started to share something with me about his journey and the reasons he made certain choices. My father was able to be transparent and unload. Today, my dad makes it a point to always show up for my sisters and me.

"Therefore, since we are surrounded by so great a cloud of witnesses [who by faith have testified to the truth of God's absolute faithfulness], stripping off every unnecessary weight and the sin which so easily and cleverly entangles us, let us run with endurance and active persistence the race that is set before us." Hebrews 12:1 (AMP)

Refuse to allow yourself to go back into environments, relationships, and activities that will cause you to become distracted or re-live your trauma.

It can be hard to know when you have found yourself in a situation that is not healthy for your healing, especially when experiencing periods of joy, acceptance, and satisfaction. You will know if you are in an unhealthy space if it brings you down, makes you feel devalued, unworthy, and unaccepted, and you cannot get enough of it.

I cannot express this enough. If you become aware that you are not safe, LEAVE! Create boundaries to keep your healing intact. Toxic relationships and behaviors will only set you back and create more pain when you have already come so far. During this time, you may seem selfish to others, especially those who have benefitted from you not knowing your value and true worth. They will be offended and not understand. If they are not willing to evolve with your newness, that is a clear indication that the season of your connection has expired for the time being.

Tool 11: Release the shame and contempt attached to your traumatic experience(s).

"Brothers, I do not consider that I have made it my own. But one thing I do: forgetting what lies behind and straining forward to what lies ahead, I press on toward the goal for the prize of the upward call of God in Christ Jesus." Philippians 3:13-14 (ESV)

"Remember not the former things, nor consider the things of old. Behold, I am doing a new thing; now it springs forth, do you not perceive it? I will make a way in the wilderness and rivers in the desert." Isaiah 43:18-19 (ESV)

When I was eighteen years old, I slept with a thirteen-year-old. Although he pursued me, he was still a minor. I was married at the time and living a life of promiscuity, struggling with my identity and confused about my destiny. We even made plans. I would get divorced so that we could get married when he turned 18 years old.

One of the first things I had to do on my healing journey was to acknowledge my abuse, so I apologized to him for abusing him. When I apologized, he did not understand; because he felt our time together was precious. I knew better.

His positive reaction still did not heal the wound. The intimacy of our relationship was unlawful in every way. I had to let go of the shame of what I had done and forgive myself. Shame can be a big stumbling block that keeps you from overcoming trauma. As you are going through the steps, there are going to be things that come up that make you feel regret, shame, and even disgust. This part of the process is necessary for your pursuit of true wholeness. Let those negative feelings go and forgive yourself.

When I was married, I got pregnant by someone else when we separated, which produced my beautiful son. Although my ex-husband and I were not together at the time that I conceived, and it was not a secret that I tried to hide, the disgrace I felt from my past still carried over into our marriage after we reconciled. Even after our divorce, there was so much resentment and shame that I felt indebted to be a certain way because of who I used to be.

Subconsciously, I believed that I owed it to specific people in my life to live low and beneath my value because of the guilt and shame that clung to me from my traumatic experiences and trauma-fueled decisions. I deserved to be emotionally and psychologically abused because of my infidelity and poor decision-making. Living like this cost me many years of joy, peace, and wholeness because I was too ashamed to share my story and get help and support.

It did not help that my parents would tell me things like, "Don't cause no problems because you know he doesn't gotta help you raise your son."

My mom's most famous quote was, "What did you do to my son? The divorce was all your fault."

Although I was her daughter, her trauma made her relationship with my ex-husband hold more value than our relationship. It felt like I was obligated never to develop, grow, continue or become because of the reality of my life's abuse and trauma.

Then one day, I said to myself, "I AM NOT LIVING LIKE THAT ANYMORE. I deserve a house, a husband, and a great paying job, and I *can* tell about the goodness of the Lord."

As I started writing my story, I began to remember things. I realized that there were many things about my character and mistakes that I had covered with shame and regret. I had buried my freedom under brokenness, my strength and abilities under fear, and my joy and integrity under people-pleasing and self-hate.

So many times throughout my journey, older people would encourage me to "Keep some stuff to yourself, baby. Everybody doesn't need to know all your business." Today, I share my experiences because if some of the people before me were not so ashamed to share, then maybe I would have been able to avoid some of the pitfalls and exploitation I experienced. What the older generation does not realize is that the younger generation longs for their transparency and honesty to help guide and strengthen us. Slavery lasted so long because we lost the power of our voice to speak the truth.

As I let go of the shame that kept me from fully walking in victory, it was like I went through the five stages of grief: denial, anger, bargaining, depression, and acceptance. I mourned my past as if it were a person, a relationship, and a loved one. Writing my story to share it with others is how I escaped the tormenting nightmares that followed me, put my past to rest, and funeralized the deeds that were haunting me.

Do not continue to wear the burden of guilt and shame on your life. Share your story and release it. Releasing it will help you to see your value and how good God has been to you.

You are not responsible for the well-being of the person who abused you. You will experience so much freedom as you share your story from a place of victory, not anger, resentment, or shame. Your past did not defeat you, so you do not have to wear it like a second skin. It is not you.

Shedding this overcoat of humiliation and self-reproach will free you to confidently walk into the person you were created to be. This allows you to put boundaries in place when people attempt to treat you like you are still the victim. You are nobody's victim, but you are an overcomer who is experiencing the newness of your life in God.

Allowing myself to be free from shame showed me that everything, the pain from my relationships with my parents, friends, and family, and even the church hurt; I had experienced all a part of God's plan to get me to a point in my life where I was truly free in Him. God placed me on a journey to deliverance, freedom, wholeness, and confidence in Him and who He created me to be. There is nothing we experience in life that is a waste, and it is for His Glory.

YOUR SPACE TO UNLOAD

CHAPTER ELEVEN

Be Accountable, Teachable, and Willing to Evolve

Your wholeness comes when you get your voice back

Some of us have to be humbled because we think of ourselves more highly than we should and are full of pride.

I had to be humbled during this journey because I thought of people more highly than God, and I had more faith in the people who supported me than in God and what He can do through anyone who trusts Him.

I knew that I was not supposed to be on this journey alone. Through my experiences searching for mentors and looking for support, I have learned to trust Him to place the right people in my path. God has answered my trust with His faithfulness and put people in my life who are properly equipped to love, nurture, and care for me through the most challenging times and the weariest of seasons.

Tool 12: Remain accountable, teachable, and always willing to evolve, continually sharing your progress and success in your journey towards wholeness.

"Therefore, confess your sins to one another and pray for one another, that you may be healed. The prayer of a righteous person has great power as it is working." James 5:16 (NIV)

"Whoever loves discipline loves knowledge, but he who hates reproof is stupid." Proverbs 12:1(NIV)

"And we impart this in words not taught by human wisdom but taught by the Spirit, interpreting spiritual truths to those who are spiritual. The natural person does not accept the things of the Spirit of God, for they are folly to him, and he is not able to understand them because they are spiritually discerned." 1 Corinthians 2:13-14 (ESV)

Blessed is the man who walks not in the counsel of the wicked, nor stands in the way of sinners, nor sits in the seat of scoffers; but his delight is in the law of the Lord, and on his law he meditates day and night. He is like a tree planted by streams of water that yields its fruit in its season, and its leaf does not wither. In all that he does, he prospers. The wicked are not so, but are like chaff that the wind drives away. Therefore the wicked will not stand in the judgment, nor sinners in the congregation of the righteous; for the Lord knows the way of the righteous, but the way of the wicked will perish." Psalm 1:1-6 (NIV)

This is not a journey that you should purposely take alone. You need direction on navigating through each step of your process and maintaining your new self-awareness and consciousness. Find someone you can trust with your heart and your mind. You must trust them to be able to receive the lessons they give and the directions you need. Sometimes this may feel like the most challenging part because of what you have experienced, but you can do it.

Pray and ask for direction when choosing the person who will help guide you, and then pay attention to their character and follow your intuition.

The people who have been assigned to you will not want to control you or box you in to become what they want or need. Their needs and desires do not trump yours.

When you identify your support person, share your progress, successes, and setbacks so that they can nurture you through the process. Keep your heart open so that you can receive the support you need. Do not become so full of yourself that you cannot learn and grow.

Be careful not to withhold areas you feel are weaknesses because they can slowly drag you back into a place of darkness and self-disgust.

The only consistent thing in the world is change. Always be willing to evolve because you need to learn more. Make sure that the people assigned to support you have space to pour into you. Be ready to pivot as situations change so you can continue to follow your purpose no matter what happens around you.

Be bold and unapologetic. This frees you and the others around you. Your wholeness comes when you get your voice back. When you can verbalize your pain, you begin to heal, and the wounds start to close. No matter what you share, do it from a place of victory instead of shame and defeat, and watch the freedom you experience. You watch what God does. It will be BEAUTIFUL!

YOUR SPACE TO UNLOAD

CHAPTER TWELVE

Be Whole

Be Loyal to Yourself First.

As an abuse survivor, I know what it feels like to walk around every day feeling broken, rejected, lost, alone and ashamed. It took years for me to find the path to overcome the trauma I experienced, and I do not want anyone else to walk through that process alone.

These 12 tools for overcoming trauma were given to help you break the chains of trauma and find wholeness in your life. This roadmap is a starting point for your journey and has been set up to assist you in getting the courage to allow yourself to launch into healing.

While you are going through the steps, there is something important that I want you to remember.

Be loyal to yourself first.

Some people have no problem doing that, but spending your life putting others' desires ahead of your own or denying your needs can cause a significant problem. It is very uncomfortable, I know. Even today, when I consciously think of my needs, I sometimes feel guilty, like I should not be doing it. But I know that it is necessary if I want to remain whole.

You deserve to be healed, and you cannot pour from an empty cup. You must value yourself the way that God values you throughout this process. Every single element and part of your story is for His Glory.

There may be setbacks, but with God's grace, support, and persistence, you will continue to walk in victory. Remember, it is important to remain accountable, be willing to grow, and let go of the unproductive behaviors, relationships, and thought patterns that have helped to hold you hostage to the trauma that you survived.

Trauma does not have the final say in your life, and God does. All you have to do is take the first step. Share your story and watch as you are propelled into your purpose after the pain of what you have experienced.

YOUR SPACE TO UNLOAD

This book does not replace the advice of a medical professional.

Scriptures taken from the Holy Bible, New International Version®, NIV®, Copyright 1973, 1978, 1984, 2011 by Biblica, Inc. Used by Permission. All rights reserved worldwide.

Scripture quotations marked (AMP) are taken from the

Amplified Bible. Copyright ©2015 by The Lockman Foundation. Used by permission.

Scripture quotations marked (ESV) are taken from the ESV

Study Bible. English Standard Version, Crossway, 2011

ISBN: 979-8-218-03552-5

Edited By: The Taylord Solution | Sherwood's Business

Center

Cover Design & Layout: Tewayne Wells BigFrameStudios | Sherwood's Business Center

Cover Photography: Everlasting Pictures

(Gale Encyclopedia of Medicine, 2008)